My First Pocket Guide

Georgia

By Carole Marsh

The GALLOPADE GANG

Carole Marsh
Bob Longmeyer
Michele Yother
Michael Marsh
Sherry Moss
Chad Beard
Sue Gentzke
Cecil Anderson

Steven Saint-Laurent
Deborah Sims
Andrew Brim
Andrea Detro
John Raines
Karin Petersen
Billie Walburn
Doug Boston

Kim Holst
Jennifer McGann
Ellen Miller
William Nesbitt, Jr
Kathy Zimmer
Wanda Coats

Published by
GALLOPADE INTERNATIONAL

www.georgiaexperience.com
800-536-2GET • www.gallopade.com

The Georgia Experience logo is a trademark of Carole Marsh and Gallopade Internat
Inc. A free catalog of The Georgia Experience Products is available by calling 800-536
or by visiting our website at www.georgiaexperience.com.

Gallopade is proud to be a member of these educational organizations and associations:

NSSEA

ASCD

SHOPA MEMBER
School, Home, & Office Products Association

Other Georgia Experience Products

- The Georgia Experience Paperback Book
- The BIG Georgia Reproducible Activity Book
- The Peachy Georgia Coloring Book
- My First Book About Georgia!
- Georgia "Jography": A Fun Run Through Our State
- Georgia Jeopardy!: Answers and Questions About Our State
- The Georgia Experience! Sticker Pack
- The Georgia Experience! Poster/Map
- Discover Georgia CD-ROM
- Georgia "Geo" Bingo Game
- Georgia "Histo" Bingo Game

A Word From the Author... (okay, a few words)...

Here's your own handy pocket guide about the great state of Georgia! It really will fit in a pocket—I tested it. And it really will be useful when you want to know a fact you forgot, to bone up for a test, or when your teacher says, "I wonder . . ." and you have the answer—instantly! Wow, I'm impressed!

Get smart, have fun!
Carole Marsh

P.S. I was born in Marietta, GA!

Georgia Basics explores your state's symbols and their special meanings!

Georgia Geography digs up the what's where in your state!

Georgia History is like traveling through time to some of your state's great moments!

Georgia People introduces you to famous personalities and your next-door neighbors!

Georgia Places shows you where you might enjoy your next family vacation!

Georgia Nature—no preservatives here, just what Mother Nature gave to Georgia!

All the real fun stuff that we just HAD to save for its own section!

Georgia
Basics

Georgia
Geography

Georgia
History

Georgia
People

Georgia
Places

Georgia
Nature

Georgia
Miscellany

Who Named You?

Georgia's official state name is...

Georgia

State Name

Word Definition

OFFICIAL: appointed, authorized, or approved by a government or organization

Georgia is one of the first states to be recognized on a commemorative quarter! Look for it in cash registers everywhere!

Statehood:
January 2, 1788

Georgia was the 4th state to ratify the U.S. Constitution, but it was the last (13th) colony to be settled!

Coccinella noemnotata is MY name (that's Latin for Lady Bug)! What's YOURS?

4

A Name of Royal Proportions!

State
Name
Origin

Georgia was named for King George II of England. In 1732 he signed a charter to create an American province that would offer unemployed English citizens a chance to begin a new life.

The oldest recorded place name in Georgia is the Appalachee River, named by the Spanish in 1528.

5

What's In A Name?

"Georgia" is not the only name by which Georgia is recognized. Like many other states, Georgia has several nicknames, official or unofficial!

State Nicknames

The Peach State

The Empire State of the South

After the Civil War, farmers developed new kinds of peaches that increased sales and made Georgia "The Peach State." The first famous peach was the Elberta.

Speaking of names, do you know the NAME of the State Song? It's *Georgia On My Mind!*

State Capital:
Atlanta

The Big "A" was Founded
1837

Official Capital Since
1868

Atlanta was founded as the southern end, or terminus, of the Western and Atlantic Railroad, and became a big transportation hub, manufacturing center, and supply depot. Atlanta was originally named Terminus (Do you see where the name came from?). In 1842, the name was changed to Marthasville in honor of Governor Wilson Lumpkin's daughter. In 1845, it finally became known as Atlanta.

The gold leaf covering the capitol's dome comes from Dahlonega–Georgia's mining town in the northeastern part of the state. Dahlonega means "precious yellow metal" (gold) in Cherokee.

Word Definition

CAPITAL: a town or city that is the official seat of government
CAPITOL: the building in which the government officials meet

Who's in Charge Here?

Georgia's has three branches:

GOVERNMENT

LEGISLATIVE EXECUTIVE JUDICIAL

State Government

The legislative branch is called the General Assembly.

TWO HOUSES: the Senate (56 members); House of Representatives (180 members)

A governor, lieutenant governor, and attorney general

SUPREME COURT with seven justices

The number of legislators is determined by population, which is counted in the census every ten years; the numbers above are certain to change as Georgia grows and prospers!

When you are 18 and register according to Georgia laws—you can vote! So please do! Your vote counts!

State Flag

The State Flag Allegiance:
*I pledge allegiance to the Georgia Flag and
to the principles for which it stands;
Wisdom, Justice, and Moderation.*

The past few years have brought growing controversy over the Confederate flag and items featuring that symbol!

The State Flag of Georgia was adopted in 1956. It is always found atop the state capitol, and all state, city, and town buildings.

State Seal

The current Great Seal was adopted by the State Constitution of 1798. In 1914, the date was changed to 1776 to correspond with the date of the Declaration of Independence.

State Seal & Motto

Word Definition

MOTTO: a sentence, phrase, or word expressing the spirits or purpose of an organization or group

State Motto

Wisdom, Justice, and Moderation

Georgia's state seal is one of the few that shows a distinctive design on both sides.

Georgia has a second state motto: "Agriculture and Commerce."

Two for the price of one! COOL!

Birds of A Feather

The state bird of Georgia is the Brown Thrasher, *Toxostoma rufum rufum*. It mimics the songs of other birds as well as singing its own.

State Bird

Brown Thrashers live in hedges and thick shrubs and come out from their dense cover to sing in the open.

Live Oak

State
Tree

The state tree of Georgia, the Live Oak, *Quercus virginiana*, is found in the Coastal Plain and is usually draped with strands of Spanish moss. It's called a "live oak" because the leaves are green year-round. The average age of these trees is said to be 300 years.

Live Oaks are known for their very hard wood. The frigate *Constitution* (Old Ironsides) and the Brooklyn Bridge were built of Georgia Live Oaks!

State Flower

CHEROKEE ROSE

Georgia's state flower is an ivory colored flower shaped like a cup with a large golden center.

State Flower

—Rosa sinnica—

You'll also see lots of kudzu *everywhere!*
Kudzu is a member of the bean family and originally came from Asia. It was brought to the South as cattle feed and to help prevent soil erosion. It can grow up to 12 inches (30 cm) each day!

You'll see the Cherokee Rose climbing, creeping, and crawling on fences and walls throughout Georgia.

13

Right Whale

The Right Whale, *Eubalaena glacialis*, is bluish-black with a lighter area on its belly. It has a stout body, a very large head, two blowholes, and no dorsal fins.

The name, "Right Whale" meant whales considered "right" for hunting. During the 1800s, they were nearly hunted to extinction, and remain rare.

RIDDLE: If the Georgia state flower got mixed up with the marine mammal, what would you have?

Answer: Right Rose–a Whale of a flower!

Knobbed Whelk

—Busycon carica—

The Knobbed Whelk, Georgia's State Shell, is tan with brown streaks on the outside and orange on the inside. It has rows of big bumps, or knobs, on the fat part of the shell. This marine snail shell grows to be 8 inches (20 cm) long, and is found all along the Georgia coast!

State Shell & Fossil

To Do List: Find out what your birthstone is. Can that gem be found in Georgia?

Shark Tooth

The shark tooth is a common fossil found in Georgia's Coastal Plain and comes in a range of colors—black, gray, white, brown, blue, and reddish-brown. In fossil form, the shark tooth can be traced back 375,000,000 years.

The shark tooth is probably one of the most sought-after fossils collected by amateur "fossilists."

It's Still the Real Thing

State Beverage

Coca-Cola is the "Unofficial" State Beverage that was invented in 1886 as a headache remedy. First year sales averaged 13 drinks a day at Jacob's Pharmacy in Atlanta where it was introduced. Today, Coca-Cola earns more than $13 billion in sales and holds four of the top five spots for best-selling soft drinks. What's your favorite?

In 1908, Coca-Cola was the first company to use the slogan, "Good to the Last Drop."

IS THIS GLASS HALF FULL OR HALF EMPTY?

You can find out everything you ever wanted to know about Coke at the World of Coca-Cola in Atlanta. You even get free samples!

How Sweet It Is

The Vidalia Sweet Onion is named for the town of Vidalia where Moses Coleman first harvested the famous vegetable in 1931. Vidalias are only properly grown in a small pocket of south Georgia, a 20-county region that provides the right soils and mild temperatures that give Vidalias their wonderfully sweet flavor.

State Vegetable

The granex seed, which produces a hot onion in other parts of the country, grows an onion you "can eat like an apple" in and around the town of Vidalia!

Make mine a chili dog WITH onions!

Vidalias are celebrated at the Vidalia Onion Festival held each year during the spring.

What'll you have with your Vidalia?

The Square Dance:

State Folk Dance

An American folk dance related to the English country dance and French ballroom dance. It includes squares, rounds, clogging, contra, line, the Virginia Reel, and heritage dances.

The Virginia Reel is an American country dance in which the partners face each other in two lines and perform various steps to the instructions of a caller.

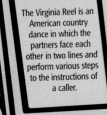

Honeybee

—Apis mellifera—

Honeybees carry pollen from flower to flower—helping them reproduce. Bees do special dances to show each other how far away flowers are—and in what direction. Do you Square Dance?

Orange and black-striped Honeybees contribute to Georgia's economy by producing honey and cross-pollinating over 50 state crops.

Largemouth Bass
—*Micropterus salmoides*—

State Fish

The Largemouth Bass is a greenish fish with a dark side stripe that lives in Georgia's quiet, vegetated lakes, ponds, and rivers.

In 1932, fisherman George Perry caught a record-breaking 22 pound, 4 ounce (10.012 kilograms) Largemouth Bass in Montgomery Lake!

Georgia Bass

Put a bass filet on foil. Drizzle with lemon juice. Sprinkle with salt and pepper. Add shredded smoked ham and broil fish until done.

Our State

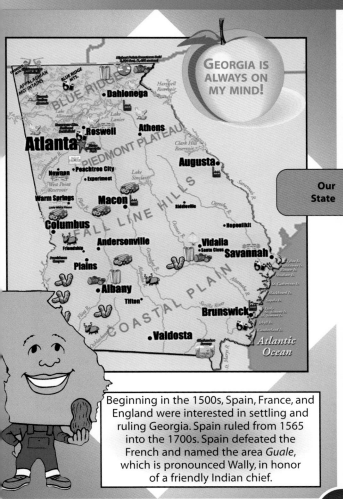

GEORGIA IS ALWAYS ON MY MIND!

Beginning in the 1500s, Spain, France, and England were interested in settling and ruling Georgia. Spain ruled from 1565 into the 1700s. Spain defeated the French and named the area *Guale*, which is pronounced Wally, in honor of a friendly Indian chief.

State Location

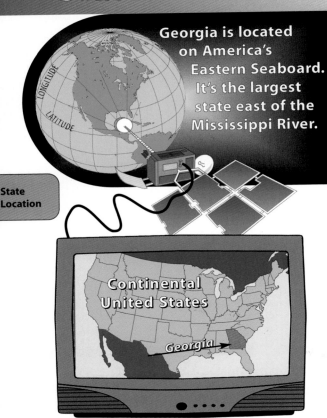

Georgia is located on America's Eastern Seaboard. It's the largest state east of the Mississippi River.

LONGITUDE

LATITUDE

State Location

Continental United States

Georgia

Word Definition

LATITUDE: Imaginary lines which run horizontally east and west around the globe
LONGITUDE: Imaginary lines which run vertically north and south around the globe.

State Neighbors

On The Border!

States: Florida   Alabama
South Carolina   Tennessee
North Carolina

Bodies of water:
Atlantic Ocean
Chattahoochee River
St. Marys River
Savannah River

State
Neighbors

You take the low road...

East–West, North–South, Area

Georgia is 250 miles (402 kilometers) east to west... or west to east. Either way, it's a long drive!

Total Area: Approx. 58,977 square miles
Land Area: Approx. 57,919 square miles

Georgia is 315 miles (507 km) north to south... or south to north. Either way, it's still a long drive!

ROAD TRIP!!

...and I'll take the high road

HIGHEST POINT

Brasstown Bald Mountain—4,784 feet above sea level (1,458 meters) where you can see panoramic views of four states: Alabama, Tennessee, North Carolina, and South Carolina.

Highest & Lowest Points

Be sure and visit Rock Eagle Effigy Mound, just north of Eatonton along Highway 441. It's a mound topped by the image of an outstretched bird with a wingspread of 120 feet (36 meters) made of milky quartz stones. It's thought to be more than five thousand years old!

LOWEST POINT
Sea Level—Along Georgia's southeastern coastline.

I'm County-ing on You

Georgia is divided into 159 counties.

Word Definition

COUNTY: an administrative subdivision of a state or territory

State Counties

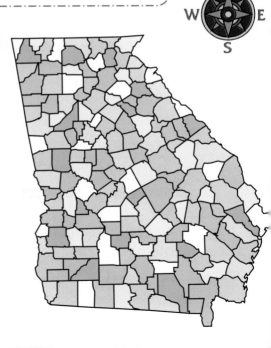

Natural Resources

Forests cover more than 2/3 of Georgia's land area

Word Definition

NATURAL RESOURCES: things that exist in or are formed by nature

Minerals:

- Clay (as in Georgia Red)
- Mica
- Bauxite
- Limestone
- Feldspar
- Marble
- Granite
- Talc
- Gold

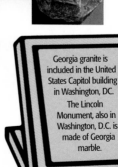

Georgia granite is included in the United States Capitol building in Washington, DC.

The Lincoln Monument, also in Washington, D.C. is made of Georgia marble.

The Fall Line Hills in central Georgia provide most of the nation's kaolin—a white, chalky clay used to manufacture paper, china, and paints.

27

Weather

Weather, Or Not?!

Georgia usually has long, hot summers, short, mild winters, and regular rainfall. The northern mountains are the coolest place to be (39°F/4°C to 78°F/26°C). The hot spot is at the beach (53°F/12°C to 81°F/27°C) on the Atlantic Ocean. Georgia has four distinct seasons—spring, summer, fall, and winter. Which is your favorite?

Weather

Highest temperature: 113°F (44°C), on May 27, 1978 at Greenville

°F=Degrees Fahrenheit °C=Degrees Cels

Lowest temperature: -17°F (-27°C), on January 27, 1940 in Floyd County

In July 1994, tropical storm Alberto roared through central and southern Georgia with 60 mile-per-hour winds and dumped 20" of rain. It caused the worst flood ever in Georgia.

NEED A MAP?

Georgia's topography includes three land areas:

NORTH: Mountains

CENTRAL: Piedmont Plateau

SOUTH: Coastal Plain (state's largest region)

THE FALL LINE HILLS (SERIES OF LOW RIDGES) separate the Piedmont Plateau from the Coastal Plain.

Word Definition

TOPOGRAPHY: the detailed mapping of the features of a small area or district

Topography

| Sea Level |
| 100 m / 328 ft |
| 200 m / 656 ft |
| 500 m / 1,640 ft |
| 1,000 m / 3,281 ft |
| 2,000 m / 6,562 ft |
| 5,000 m / 16,404 ft |

The Piedmont Plateau is the most densely populated region. About 60% of Georgians live here.

Back on Top

Mountains-Some you might like to climb!

- Brasstown Bald Mountain
- Lookout Mountain
- Stone Mountain
- Pigeon Mountain
- Blood Mountain
- Chestnut Mountain
- Chunky Gal Mountain

Ranges

- Appalachian
- Blue Ridge

On top of Old Smokey...

Down the River

Some of the best summer fun you can have is "tubing" down the "Hooch"— the Chattahoochee River, that is!

TUBULAR!!

These are some of the rivers of Georgia—some *wild and wooly*—some gently rolling... and flowing to the Atlantic Ocean or the Gulf of Mexico.

Major Rivers

- Savannah
- Ogeechee
- Ocmulgee
- Oconee
- Altamaha
- Chattooga
- Suwannee

Did you notice how many Georgia rivers have Indian names?

- St. Marys
- Chattahoochee
- Flint
- Etowah
- Satilla
- Tugaloo
- Seneca

Hey, how about some Famous Springs, too?

Major Lakes & Reservoirs

- **HARTWELL RESERVOIR**
- **CLARK HILL RESERVOIR**
- **WEST POINT RESERVOIR**
  - **LAKE ALLATOONA**
  - **LAKE OCONEE**
  - **LAKE SINCLAIR**
- **LAKE LANIER**
- **LITHIA SPRINGS**
- **CAVE SPRING**
- **JAY BIRD SPRINGS**
- **WARM SPRINGS**

The bubbling waters of Georgia's many springs have long been thought to have healing powers. In the 1800s, Lithia Springs became a popular health spa. President Franklin D. Roosevelt built a home in Warm Springs because he thought the nearby springs would help his legs, which were paralyzed from a disease called polio.

Word Definition

RESERVOIR: a body of water stored for public use

Cities & Towns

ARE YOU A CITY MOUSE... OR A COUNTRY MOUSE?

Have you heard these wonderful Georgia city, town, and crossroad names? Perhaps you can start your own collection!

Cities & Towns

LARGER CITIES:
Atlanta (capital)
Columbus
Savannah (oldest)
Macon
Albany
Roswell
Athens
Augusta
Marietta
Warner Robins

OTHER TOWNS:
Ideal
Plains (home of
    Jimmy Carter)
Hiawassee
Ducktown
Santa Claus
Flowery Branch
Thunderbolt
Tallapoosa
Hopeulikit
Rising Fawn
Ochlockonee
Peachtree City (home of
    Gallopade International–
    hey, that's us!)

Transportation

Major Interstate Highways
I-75, I-85, I-95
I-16, I-20, I-185
In northeast Atlanta, I-85 and I-285 intersect to form a 'twisty-tangly' maze of highways known as Spaghetti Junction.

Transportation

Railroads
About 5,000 miles (8,000 kilometers) of track serve some 500 Georgia communities– providing access to the largest rail system in the Southeast.

Atlanta has another train–MARTA (Metropolitan Atlanta Rapid Transit Authority)–a high-speed commuter train that runs through downtown Atlanta and out to the 'burbs. It carries about 200,000 passengers daily!

Major Airport
Atlanta's Hartsfield Int'l Airport has the world's largest terminal and serves more than 73,000,000 passengers a year.

Seaports
- Savannah
- Brunswick
- St. Marys

History Timeline

1540	Spanish expedition led by de Soto enters Georgia
1732	King George II of England grants charter for colony
1733	Oglethorpe & English settlers arrive, found Savannah
1750	Slave trade allowed in Georgia
1775	Revolutionary War begins
1776	Declaration of Independence signed
1777	First state constitution ratified
1788	Georgia is 4th state to ratify the U.S Constitution
1826	Creek Indians forced to cede last of land and move
1838	Cherokees forced out on "Trail of Tears"
1861	Georgia secedes from Union
1864	General Sherman "burns" through Georgia
1865	Civil War ends; slavery abolished; secession repealed
1877	New state constitution; Atlanta is permanent capital
1945	President Roosevelt dies at Warm Springs
1969	Federal District Court orders racially balanced schools
1996	Georgia hosts Summer Olympics

History Timeline

On to the
21st
century!

"THERE'S GOLD IN THEM THAR HILLS!"

In 1828, gold was discovered in Dahlonega and started America's first gold rush!

Here come the humans!

As early as 8000 B.C., Mound Builders inhabited Georgia. Beside rivers and streams, they built pyramids flattened at the top that were as high as 60 feet (18 meters). These pyramids were made of dirt or piled shells and sometimes in the form of rings or circles. Tribal towns flourished in the shadows of these man-made hills for centuries.

Early History

Archaeologists aren't sure whether the mounds were used as places of worship, burial grounds, or lookouts.

What do you think they were used for?

You can still see some of these mounds today, including Etowah Mounds near Cartersville, Ocmulgee National Monument near Macon, and Kolomoki Mounds in southwestern Georgia.

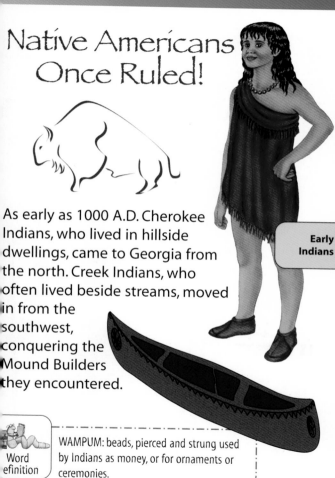

Native Americans Once Ruled!

As early as 1000 A.D. Cherokee Indians, who lived in hillside dwellings, came to Georgia from the north. Creek Indians, who often lived beside streams, moved in from the southwest, conquering the Mound Builders they encountered.

Early Indians

Word Definition

WAMPUM: beads, pierced and strung used by Indians as money, or for ornaments or ceremonies.

Land Ho

In March of 1540, Spaniard Hernando de Soto and 600 soldiers marched inland from the Gulf of Mexico to Georgia in search of fabulous cities of gold. Riding on horses and

Early Explorers

dressed in metal armor and helmets, these *conquistadores* must have impressed the Indians they met.

De Soto and his men looked and looked, but never found the wonderful cities of gold. He died of fever in 1542. Do you think it was *gold fever*?

Colonization

Home, Sweet, Home

In 1730, Parliament member James Oglethorpe was very concerned about England's horrible unemployment. He and 20 other important men sent a request to King George II asking for a charter of land—a colony in the New World of America that would offer these folks a chance for a new life. It would be named Georgia in the King's honor.

Colonization

In 1732, the king granted the request. Oglethorpe and 35 families set sail on the *Anne* for the New World and a new life. They landed at Yamacraw Bluff and started looking for a good place to settle. After rowing a short distance up the Savannah River, Oglethorpe and his guide, Colonel William Bull, met a group of Yamacraw Indians. They talked with the *mico*, or chief, named Tomochichi, who said it would be OK for the settlers to stay.

On February 12, 1733, Oglethorpe and his band of English settlers pitched their tents and started the city of Savannah.

Oglethorpe carefully laid out the street design for Savannah. It's the first "planned" city in the U.S.

The Three Ps= Peaches, Peanuts, and Pecans

The Spanish brought peach plants with them to the New World. They were first grown in Georgia in the 1700s. Since then it's been nothing but peaches, peaches, peaches. After the Civil War, peach growers developed wonderful new types that boosted the peach industry and made Georgia the "Peach State." Georgia remains one of the leading producers of the luscious fruit– growing about 40 different kinds today!

Key Crop/Product

There are 61 streets in Atlanta that have "peachtree" in the name.

What a Peach of a name—and what a way to get lost!

Georgia leads the nation in the production of peanuts (top cash crop) and pecans. About ½ of the peanuts (about 800 billion a year) and ⅓ of pecans are grown here. Georgia is also a leading producer of chickens and eggs. Gainesville is the "Poultry Capital of the World!"

Fact...or Fiction?

- In the north Georgia Mountains, a sad tale of unrequited love unfolds...Sautee was a Chickasaw brave and Nacoochee was a Cherokee Indian princess. The two tribes were at war, so the couple were not supposed to be together. They loved each other so much, they were willing to do anything—so they ran off together. They came back to plead for peace between the two tribes. Nacoochee's father had Sautee thrown from a cliff to his death. Nacoochee, not able to live without her love, jumped off the cliff to be with him forever. Grief-stricken, Nacoochee's father realized how much they loved each other and buried them together in the mound you'll find outside of the north Georgia mountain town of Helen.

Legends & Lore

- Ever heard of the Goat Man of Dixie? For over 50 years, he traveled the backroads of the Deep South, delighting children with his tales of outlaws and Indians, bears and mountain lions. His traveling companions were a herd of goats. His pioneering spirit reminded children of Davy Crockett and Daniel Boone. In the late '80s, he was rumored to be 108!

> Rock Star Elton John is now an "honorary" native of Atlanta. That makes him an official Georgia Peach.
>
> The famous rock star now has a home in the capital city.

OF HUMAN BONDAGE

Bans on slavery and private ownership of land were part of the original laws set up by the Georgia trustees. These laws were very unpopular, and in 1750, were changed and slave trade was allowed.

While not all farmers owned slaves, some plantation owners could only enlarge their farms with slave labor. Abolitionists were against slavery. Over time, slaves rebelled. Some people helped blacks escape slavery on the Underground Railroad, a route to the northern states where they could live freely.

Slaves and Slavery

The issue of slavery and states' rights led to the Civil War.

In 1863, the Emancipation Proclamation, issued by U.S. President Abraham Lincoln, freed the slaves in areas still under Confederate control.

Freedom!

After the Georgia colony had been established for about 40 years, some colonists felt that the royal governors ignored their ideas and concerns. As time went by, more and more colonists wanted to be independent from British rule. In 1775, the colonies went to war with England. On July 4, 1776, the Declaration of Independence was signed.

Revolution

At the Battle of Rice Boats, fought March 1776 in Savannah, Americans burned British ships and the British stole about 1,600 barrels of the colonists' rice.

Brother

The Civil War was fought between the American states. The argument was over the right of the states to make their own decisions, including whether or not to own slaves. Some of the southern states began to secede (leave) the Union. They formed the Confederate States of America. In 1861, Georgia became the fifth state to leave the Union and join ten other states in the Confederacy.

The Civil War!

Word Definition

RECONSTRUCTION: the recovery and rebuilding period following the Civil War.

vs. Brother

Many Civil War battles were fought in Georgia. Soldiers often found themselves fighting their former friends and neighbors, even relatives. Georgia provided nearly 125,000 troops during the war. After four long years, the Confederacy surrendered at Appomattox Court House in Virginia.

The Civil War!

More Americans were killed during the Civil War than during World Wars I and II!

Get It In Writing!

The Charter for a Corporation entitled The Trustee for Establishing the Colony of Georgia in America, 1732

The Georgia State Constitution, 1777, 1877, 1945, 1976

Famous Documents

Declaration of Independence, 1776, written by Thomas Jefferson; signed by Georgians Lyman Hall, George Walton, and Button Gwinnett

U.S. Constitution, 1787, written by James Madison

U.S. Constitution, 1789, went into effect

Immigrants

WELCOME TO AMERICA!

People have come to Georgia from other states and many other countries on almost every continent! As time has gone by, Georgia's population has grown more diverse. This means that people of different races and from different cultures and ethnic backgrounds have moved to Georgia.

Immigrants

In the past, many immigrants came to Georgia from England, Austria, Germany, Scotland, Wales, Italy, Switzerland, and other European countries. Slaves migrated (involuntarily) from Africa. More recently, people have migrated to Georgia from South American and Asian countries. Only a certain number of immigrants are allowed to move to America each year. Many of these immigrants eventually become U.S. citizens.

Disasters & Catastrophes

1838

U.S. Federal troops forced the Cherokee to leave Georgia; 4,000 died along the "Trail of Tears" in the march westward.

1864

Horror in Andersonville–this famous camp is considered to be the deadliest prison in Civil War history!

1946

Disasters & Catastrophes!

In one of the country's worst fires, 119 people were killed when the 15-story Winecoff Hotel on Peachtree Street in Atlanta was destroyed by fire

1994

On December 20, 1893, Georgia became the first state to enact a law against lynching. It was designed to prevent mob violence.

The worst natural disaster in Georgia occurred when torrential rains from tropical storm Alberto caused the Flint River to flood and rampage through the southwestern part of the state. In Albany, unearthed coffins floated through the flooded streets. The flood submerged an area the size of Massachusetts and Rhode Island combined! More than 30 people lost their lives.

Legal Stuff

1845

Georgia organized its first Supreme Court.

1870

Georgia ratified the 14th and 15th Amendments to the Constitution and was readmitted to the United States.

1914

Sixth District Federal Reserve Bank was established in Atlanta.

1943

Georgia became the first state to allow 18 year-olds the right to vote.

1969

Federal District Court ordered racially balanced schools.

Georgia Women

1836

Wesleyan College (Georgia Female College) became world's first chartered to grant degrees to women only.

1866

Georgia became the first state to extend full property rights to married women.

Georgia Women

1915

Women were first allowed to practice law in Georgia courts.

1919

Georgia became the first state to reject the 19th Amendment giving women the right to vote.

1920

Women gained suffrage nationally and began voting in Georgia for the first time.

Word Definition

SUFFRAGE: the right or privilege of voting

Fight!, Fight!, Fight!

Wars that Georgians fought in:

- **Revolutionary War**
- **War of 1812**
- **Mexican War**
- **Civil War**
- **Spanish-American War**
- **World War I**
- **World War II**
- **Korean War**
- **Vietnam War**
- **Persian Gulf War**

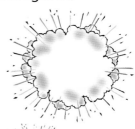

Wars

Claim to Fame

How 'bout them Braves!

Claim to Fame

In 1966, the Milwaukee Braves moved to Atlanta. In 1975, media mogul and sports team owner, Ted Turner purchased the baseball club. Two years later, during a long losing streak, he thought he'd try managing the club–that was short lived–the losing streak came to an end too! In 1991, with Manager Bobby Cox, the Braves went from worst in their division to first! Their winning ways continued and in 1995, the Atlanta Braves won the World Series! In the 1990s, they won their division every year and went on to win the National League pennant five times.

Indian Tribes

➺ Cherokee
➺ Creek
 • Coweta
 • Chehaw
 • Yamacraw
➺ Yamasee

• Georgia's Cherokees spoke the Iroquoian language.
• Creek, an alliance of different groups, is short for Ochessee Creek, where these people settled.

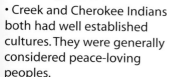

• Creek and Cherokee Indians both had well established cultures. They were generally considered peace-loving peoples.
• The Yamasee, who inhabited the coastal area, revolted against the European intruders.

Indian Tribes

The Cherokee Indians were the largest of the civilized tribes in the Southeast. They, and the Creek, supported the British during the Revolutionary War.

Here, There, Everywhere!

HERNANDO DE SOTO, from Spain, was first European to explore Georgia

SIR FRANCIS DRAKE, English explorer, plundered Spanish missions along the Georgia coast

Explorers & Settlers

JOHN CHARLES FREMONT, Georgian who explored much of the area between the Rocky Mountains and the Pacific Ocean

GENERAL JAMES OGLETHORPE, a member of the English Parliament, is considered to be the Father of Georgia

State Founders

These people played important roles in the creation of our state and our Nation!

Founding Fathers

JAMES OGLETHORPE—Georgia's Founding Father

BUTTON GWINNETT—signed the Declaration of Independence; member of the Continental Congress; acting Governor

JOSEPH HABERSHAM—member of Georgia convention to ratify the United States Constitution; member of the Continental Congress; United States Postmaster General

LYMAN HALL—signed the Declaration of Independence on behalf of Georgia; member of the Continental Congress; Governor

GEORGE WALTON—signed the Declaration of Independence and Articles of Confederation on behalf of Georgia; Governor

ALEXANDER H. STEPHENS—Vice-President of the Confederacy; Governor

Founding Mothers

State Founders

MARY MUSGROVE—Creek Indian leader, trader; became General Oglethorpe's interpreter and representative among the Indians; influenced the Creek to remain loyal to the British during the conflict with Spain for control of Georgia.

NANCY HART—Legendary Georgia Patriot known for her courage in fighting the British troops. Legend has it that Nancy and her husband Benjamin provided refuge for patriots in their cabin in the north Georgia woods near Elberton.

Among the first British to set sail on the *Anne* for the new colony of Georgia were: 2 merchants, 5 carpenters, 2 wig makers, 5 farmers, 1 gardener, 1 upholsterer, 1 baker, 1 miller, 1 surgeon, and 1 writer.

HENRY MacNEAL TURNER–civil rights leader, Union chaplain for black troops in Civil War; served two terms in Georgia assembly.

MARTIN LUTHER KING, JR.–born in Atlanta, clergyman, civil rights leader, brilliant orator; believed that ALL Americans should have equal rights. Worked for social change through non-violent means; founded the Southern Christian Leadership Conference; is remembered for his stirring speech, "I Have A Dream"; won Nobel Peace Prize; was assassinated in 1968 in Memphis; a federal holiday on the 3rd Monday in January honors his birthday.

Famous African-Americans

WALTER FRANCIS WHITE–author, civil rights leader; secretary of the National Association for the Advancement of Colored People.

CORETTA SCOTT-KING–wife of Martin Luther King, Jr.; continued her husband's mission after his death.

ALONZO F. HERNDON–Atlanta's first black millionaire; a former slave; opened barber shop; then, founded Atlanta Mutual Insurance Company.

Ghosts

DID SOMEONE SAY BOO!?

- **The Ghostly Lord of LaFayette Square, Savannah**
- **Mary the Wanderer, St. Simons Island**
- **The Doctor's Ghost, Crescent**
- **"Baby Jane" of Orange Hall, St. Marys**
- **The Polo Player of Cumberland Island**
- **The Girl the Nuns Loved, Tybee Island**
- **The Pink Lady, Atlanta**
- **Two Young Lovers, Roswell**
- **The Golden-Haired Child, Stone Mountain**
- **A Ghost in the "Uncle Remus" House, Atlanta**
- **Miss Mary, Grantville**
- **The Phantom of Andersonville**
- **The Georgia Werewolf, Talbot County**
- **Confederate Soldiers in the Mist, Washington**
- **The Lady of the Library, Gainesville**

Redbird, a Cherokee Indian Chief, is buried near the railroad tracks in Dalton. His spirit is said to haunt the railroad, and many train wrecks have occurred in this area!

Sports Figures

TY COBB–professional baseball player, nicknamed the Georgia Peach; had highest career batting average of .367

JACKIE ROBINSON–professional baseball; first black player in major leagues

BOBBY JONES–great golfer, won many tournaments, founded The Masters Golf Tournament

JIM BROWN–First National Football player to rush more than 10,000 yards

WALT FRAZIER– Basketball Hall of Famer

GWEN TORRENCE–Won most track medals (3) at 1992 Summer Olympics in Barcelona, Spain

EVANDER HOLYFIELD–Heavy-weight Boxing Champion

TERESA EDWARDS–In 1992, became first U.S. basketball player–male or female–to compete in three Olympic Games. Two of the teams won gold medals!

Entertainers

★ SPIKE LEE–film-maker

★ JULIA ROBERTS–actress

★ HOLLY HUNTER–actress

★ DEFOREST KELLEY–actor; "Dr. Leonard McCoy" on *Star Trek*

★ OLIVER HARDY–comedian; one of the Laurel and Hardy duo

★ JOANNE WOODWARD–actress

★ RAY CHARLES–singer

★ SAMUEL L. JACKSON–actor

★ TRISHA YEARWOOD–country singer

★ JAMES BROWN–R&B singer

★ JESSYE NORMAN– opera singer

Entertainers

★ ALAN JACKSON–country singer

★ JEFF FOXWORTHY–comedian

★ SHAWN MULLINS–rock singer

★ MUSICAL GROUPS–REM, Collective Soul, B-52s, the Allman Brothers Band, Gladys Knight and the Pips

RIDDLE: Which person on the list above says, "You may be a Redneck if…"?

Answer: Jeff Foxworthy

Authors

PENS ARE MIGHTIER THAN SWORDS!

- LEWIS GRIZZARD–humorist
- JOEL CHANDLER HARRIS–"Uncle Remus"; his home in Atlanta, the Wren's Nest, was opened to the public–making it the first house museum in the city
- MARGARET MITCHELL–author of *Gone With the Wind*, Pulitzer Prize Winner
- JAMES DICKEY–novelist, poet
- FERROL SAMS–physician and author
- CELESTINE SIBLEY–columnist
- EUGENIA PRICE–novelist
- ANNE RIVERS SIDDONS–novelist
- ALICE WALKER–won Pulitzer Prize for *The Color Purple*

- HENRY W. GRADY–journalist, editor
- ERSKINE CALDWELL–novelist
- SIDNEY LANIER–poet; best known for "The Marshes of Glynn"
- FLANNERY O'CONNOR– novel
- RALPH EMERSON MCGILL– editor and publisher

Gone With the Wind, the best-selling novel ever written, has been translated into 36 different languages.

Nom de plume: French for per name, a fictitious name under which a writer chooses to write instead of his or her real name

60

Artists

EDWARD O. MARTIN–folk art

HOWARD FINSTER–folk art

ULYSSES S. DAVIS–wood carver

LEROY ALMON–wood carver

LANIER MEADERS–potter

LUCINDA TOOMER–quilter

SERANDA VESPERMANN–glass sculptures

WALT KELLY–cartoonist, creator of the "Pogo" comic strip about characters who live in the Okefenokee Swamp. It highlights environmental problems, and still runs in about 200 newspapers. There's even an annual Pogofest in Waycross.

Georgia's folk life play, *Swamp Gravy*, portrays the life of rural folks–with some exaggerations added. The play, staged in Colquitt, changes every year.

EDUCATORS & TEACHER

MARTHA McCHESNEY BERRY–founded Berry College (world's largest college campus)

LUCY LANEY–founded a private school for blacks in Augusta which became the Haines Norm and Industrial Institute

DAVID (DEAN) RUSK–professor, U.S. State Departmen official; helped establish the Marshall Plan

JOSEPH SEQUOYAH–Cherokee scholar; invented a written alphabet based on sounds of his native language

ELIOT WIGGINTON–teacher and creator of the *Foxfire* series which began as a project for his class at the Rabun Gap-Nacoochee School. The series explored the rich heritage of the northeast Georgia mountair

Educators & Scientists

DOCTORS AND INVENTORS

CRAWFORD W. LONG–surgeon, first physician to use ether as an anesthetic

ELI WHITNEY–inventor; developed the cotton gin, a labor-saving device that made cotton "King" in the south

RIDDLE: What you do call an anesthetized rabbit?

Answer: An Ether Bunny!

Military Figures

SOLDIERS

NATHANAEL GREENE– Revolutionary War general; successfully commanded the army of the South against the British

JOHN BROWN GORDON– Confederate army general; U.S. Senator; governor of Georgia

WILLIAM JOSEPH HARDEE–fought in the Mexican War; Confederate Army brigadier-general

COURTNEY HICKS HODGES–rose from rank of private to four-star general; commanded the American First Army in World War II

JAMES MOORE WAYNE–soldier, politician, Georgia circuit court judge; U.S. Representative, associate justice

Military Figures

LUCIUS DuBIGNON CLAY–commander in chief of U.S. armed forces in Europe and military governor of U.S. military zone in Germany during World War II; oversaw Berlin Airlift

The famous Polish patriot and U.S. Colonial Officer, Count Casimir Pulaski, died in Georgia in a valiant attempt to regain Savannah from the British in 1779. Fort Pulaski National Monument near Savannah was named in the Count's honor.

GOOD GUYS/GALS

- **Juliette Gordon Low**–founder of the Girl Scouts of America
- **Rebecca Latimer Felton**–author, political reformer; first woman United States senator when she served one day as an interim appointee
- **"Doc" Holliday**–(*Good Guy/Bad Guy*) John Henry "Doc" Holliday is remembered as one of the men who stood beside Wyatt Earp at the famous shoot-out at the OK Corral in Tombstone, Arizona.
- **William B. Hartsfield**–one of Atlanta's most noted mayors, was famous for his quote, "The city too busy to hate." Atlanta's busy airport bears his name–Hartsfield Atlanta International Airport.

Good Guys & Bad Guys

BAD GUYS

- Edward Teach–better known as **Blackbeard the Pirate,** attacked ships along the Georgia coast during the early 1700s.
- **Frank Dupree**–last person hung in Atlanta on September 1, 1922. He'd killed a detective during a jewelry store robbery. He asked that his hair be combed back before the hood was put over his head. About 5,000 people watched the hanging.

Political Leaders

- James Earl (Jimmy) Carter–39th U.S. president
- Roy Barnes–elected governor of Georgia in 1998
- Clarence Thomas– Supreme Court Justice
- John Ross–Cherokee chief
- William McIntosh–Creek chief
- Cynthia McKinney–first African-American congresswoman from Georgia
- Andrew Young–civil rights leader, politician
- Robert A. Toombs–politician, secretary of state of the Confederacy
- Cathy Cox, Secretary of State
- Samuel (Sam) Nunn–U.S. Senator; Senate Steering Committee
- Maynard Jackson–first African-American mayor of Atlanta
- Grace T. Hamilton–first African-American woman elected to Georgia House of Representatives
- Leroy R. Johnson–first African-American Georgia state senator

Political Leaders

...sident Franklin D. Roosevelt's "Little White House" is in Warm Springs. Children in the area knew him as "Uncle Rosey."

Keeping the Fait

Old Kiokee Baptist Church—near Appling, the oldest Baptist church in Georgia, was established in 1771.

Springfield Baptist Church—is the nation's oldest independent African-American congregation. It was founded in 1787 when slaves came with their masters from South Carolina during the Revolutionary War. Reverend Kelly Lowe is buried here. He organized the first Sunday School classes for blacks in the U.S.

SCHOOLS

Some of Georgia's colleges and universities:

♦ University of Georgia, Athens
♦ Georgia Technical Institute, Atlanta
♦ Georgia State University, Atlanta
♦ Morehouse College, Atlanta
♦ LaGrange College—oldest independen college
♦ Kennesaw State University
♦ Morris Brown College, Atlanta
♦ Spelman College, Atlanta
♦ State University of West Georgia, Carrollton
♦ Emory University, Atlanta
♦ Savannah School of Art and Desig
♦ Georgia Southern University, Statesboro

Churches and Schools

Georgia's first public school system was established in 1870.

Historic Sites and Parks

HISTORIC SITES

★ Andersonville National Historic Site
★ Kolomoki Mounds State Park–National Historic Landmark
★ Atlanta History Center–includes the Tullie Smith

House, an 1840s working farm, the 1928 Swan House, and the Atlanta History Museum

PARKS

★ Kennesaw Mountain Battlefield National Park
★ Chickamauga and Chattanooga National Military Park. Established in 1890, it's the oldest and largest military park in the nation.
★ Fort Mountain State Park (with prehistoric, man-made defense wall)
★ Franklin D. Roosevelt State Park–largest state park in Georgia
★ Black Rock Mountain State Park–near Clayton

Historic Sites and Parks

is the highest state park
★ Providence Canyon State Conservation Park–Georgia's "Little Grand Canyon"
★ Indian Springs State Park–first state park in Georgia–commemorates

821 treaty between the Creek Nation and the U.S.

Early Residency

★ Chief Vann House–Chatsworth mansion of Cherokee Chief Joseph Vann, now called the "Showplace of the Cherokee Nation"

★ Bulloch Hall–Roswell home of U.S. President Teddy Roosevelt's mother, Mittie Bulloch Roosevelt

★ Newnan–the "City of Homes" was a neutral hospital zone during the Civil War which spared a lot of historical homes and other buildings. You can tour the beautiful antebellum mansions in the spring and fall.

Home, Sweet Home!

★ Isaiah Davenport House–saved from the wrecking ball in 1955, was Savannah's first preservation effort. More than 2,000 structures have been designated as historically or architecturally significant in Savannah.

★ Tara–fictional antebellum home of Scarlet O'Hara in Margaret Mitchell's *Gone With the Wind*. Mitchell wrote her famous novel in an apartment on Crescent Avenue in Atlanta that she nicknamed "The Dump," which is now a popular tourist site with international visitors!

Battles and Forts

A few of Georgia's famous **Battles and Forts**

- **Battle of Bloody Marsh–Fort Frederica on St. Simons Island (ended Spain's claim to Georgia)**
- **Battle of Rice Boats–Savannah (during Revolutionary War)**
- **Kennesaw Mountain (Confederate victory during Civil War under leadership of General Joseph E. Johnston)**
- **Chickamauga Creek (northwestern Georgia–bloodiest two days of the Civil War)**
- **On September 2, 1864, Union General William Sherman and 60,000 troops marched into Atlanta and began an attack that stunned the South. He and his troops torched Atlanta, leaving only 400 of the city's 3,800 buildings standing. He then began his infamous "March to the Sea" and headed his troops toward Savannah, burning and looting a 60-mile-wide (96 kilometers) path of destruction.**
- **Blood Mountain (site of a major battle between Cherokee and Creek Indians)**

On April 16, 1865, Fort Tyler became the last Confederate fort to fall. It fell to Maj. Gen. James H. Wilson—a week after the war ended!

Libraries

- THE ATLANTA-FULTON COUNTY PUBLIC LIBRARY (STATE'S LARGEST PUBLIC LIBRARY)
- LIBRARY OF THE UNIVERSITY OF GEORGIA (STATE'S LARGEST ACADEMIC LIBRARY), Athens
- THE GEORGIA STATE HISTORICAL LIBRARY, Atlanta
- THE CARTER PRESIDENTIAL LIBRARY—PART OF THE CARTER CENTER, Atlanta
- Georgia's first library was established in Savannah in 1736

Libraries

The Margaret Mitchell Library in Fayetteville has a large collection of Civil War works. Do you remember which book this library's namesake wrote?

Answer: Gone With the Wind

Zoos & Attractions

- **ZOO ATLANTA**
- **WHITEWATER / AMERICAN ADVENTURES** (FUN PARKS FOR KIDS IN MARIETTA)
- **CUMBERLAND ISLAND NATIONAL SEASHORE**
- **SIX FLAGS OVER GEORGIA,** Austell
- **FERNBANK SCIENCE CENTER AND PLANETARIUM,** Atlanta
- **BABYLAND GENERAL–HOME OF THE CABBAGE PATCH DOLLS,** Cleveland
- **CALLAWAY GARDENS,** Pine Mountain
- **ATLANTA INTERNATIONAL SPEEDWAY,** Hampton
- **AUGUSTA NATIONAL GOLF COURSE–HOME OF THE MASTERS GOLF TOURNAMENT**
- **OKEFENOKEE NATIONAL WILDLIFE REFUGE**
- **STONE MOUNTAIN PARK,** Atlanta
- **STATE BOTANICAL GARDEN OF GEORGIA,** Athens
- **CENTENNIAL OLYMPIC PARK,** Atlanta
- **CHATTAHOOCHEE RIVER NATIONAL RECREATION AREA**
- **SCITREK,** Atlanta (one of the nation's top 10 science centers with interactive exhibits)
- **CABLE NEWS NETWORK (CNN) CENTER,** Atlanta

LION

Museums

- HIGH MUSEUM OF ART, Atlanta
- HARRIET TUBMAN AFRICAN-AMERICAN MUSEUM, Columbus

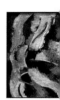

- ROAD TO TARA MUSEUM, Atlanta
- MARTIN LUTHER KING, JR. CENTER, Atlanta
- FERNBANK MUSEUM OF NATURAL HISTORY, Atlanta
- MUSEUM OF ARTS AND SCIENCES, Macon
- GEORGIA MOUNTAINS HISTORY MUSEUM, Gainesville
- TELFAIR ACADEMY OF ARTS AND SCIENCES, Savannah
- UNCLE REMUS MUSEUM AND PARK, Eatonton
- WARNER ROBINS AIR FORCE MUSEUM
- CONFEDERATE NAVAL MUSEUM, Columbus (has remains of the CSS *Chattahoochee* and the CSS *Jackson/Muscogee*–two Confederate gunboats)
- NATIONAL INFANTRY MUSEUM, Columbus
- GOLD MUSEUM, Dahlonega
- CRAWFORD W. LONG MUSEUM, Jefferson
- NATIONAL COUNTRY MUSIC MUSEUM, Buena Vista
- GEORGIA MUSEUM OF ART, Athens

Museums

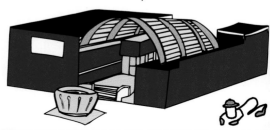

Monuments & Places

MONUMENTS

• **FORT FREDERICA NATIONAL MONUMENT**—THE MOST IMPORTANT OF GEORGIA'S EARLY SETTLEMENTS. FROM THIS LOCATION, GEORGIANS COULD WATCH THE SPANISH TO SEE WHAT THEY WERE UP TO, AND ESTABLISH ENGLAND'S CLAIM TO GEORGIA'S COAST. THE COLONIAL VICTORY AT FORT FREDERICA ENDED SPAIN'S CLAIM TO GEORGIA, **St. Simons Island.**

• **OCMULGEE NATIONAL MONUMENT**—683 ACRE (273 HECTARES) SITE PRESERVES THE REMAINS OF MOUND BUILDERS THAT LIVED IN THIS AREA BETWEEN 10,000 B.C. AND EARLY A.D. 1700s, **near Macon.**

• **Stone Mountain** (near Atlanta) is one of the world's largest exposed granite rocks. It rises 830 feet (249 meters) and covers 2 square miles (5.2 square kilometers). A carving of Jefferson Davis, General Robert E. Lee, and General "Stonewall" Jackson graces the northern face. You can take a tram up—up—up to the very top of the mountain, or you can put your hiking shoes on and walk all the way! Visit between Memorial Day and Labor Day and see an exciting laser and sound show with really great fireworks!

Monuments & Places

73

The Arts

- **WOODRUFF ARTS CENTER** (HOME OF THE ATLANTA SYMPHONY, ATLANTA COLLEGE OF ART, AND ALLIANCE THEATRE), Atlanta
- **CENTER FOR PUPPETRY ARTS**, Atlanta
- **ATLANTA OPERA**
- **THE ATLANTA BALLET**–the oldest ballet company in the United States
- **FOX THEATER**–BUILT IN 1928 AS A SHRINE TEMPLE; LISTED ON THE NATIONAL REGISTER OF HISTORICAL PLACES, Atlanta; HAS THE 2ND LARGEST THEATRE ORGAN, THE MOLLER, IN U.S.
- **THE POETRY SOCIETY OF GEORGIA**
- **Springer Opera House**, Columbus, Georgia's official State Theatre
- **Cyclorama** in Grant Park, a painting & diorama of the Battle of Atlanta, is 400 feet (120 meters) in circumference. It's a 3-D panorama!

The Arts

To be... or not to be… involved in the arts—that is the question. What is your *final* answer?

SEASHORES

- Georgia's Atlantic coastline stretches 100 miles (160 km) south from the Savannah River down to the St. Marys River!
- Georgia's Golden Isles are Ossabaw, Wassaw, St. Catherines, St. Simons, Jekyll, Sea, Sapelo, and Cumberland.
- Cumberland Island National Seashore– the largest of the barrier islands.

The Atlantic Intracoastal Waterway weaves its way through the state's coastal islands.

Seashores & Lighthouses

LIGHTHOUSES

The candy-cane striped Sapelo Lighthouse is one of Georgia's five remaining lighthouses. They have helped sailors navigate the waters of Georgia's Golden Isles for more than 150 years!

TRAILS

THE APPALACHIAN TRAIL—the world's longest continuous mountain trail is 2,150 miles (3,440 kilometers) and runs through 14 states. It begins in Maine at Mount Katahdin and weaves its way southward to Springer Mountain in northeast Georgia.

ROADS

PEACHTREE STREET, PEACHTREE ROAD, WEST PEACHTREE, PEACHTREE INDUSTRIAL BOULEVARD, PEACHTREE CORNERS, NORTHEAST PEACHTREE, PEACHTREE PARKWAY, PEACHTREE BATTLE, PEACHTREE CENTER AVENUE AND SO ON AND SO ON!

BRIDGES—COVERED, THAT IS!

Trails, Roads, & Bridges!

Covered bridges are romantic reminders of Georgia's horse-and-buggy days (way before you were born)!

Here are some you can still visit:

- **Auchumpkee Covered Bridge,** THOMASTON
- **LOWERY COVERED BRIDGE,** GEORGIA'S OLDEST, CARTERSVILLE
- **STOVALL COVERED BRIDGE,** SAUTEE ▷
- **BIG RED OAK CREEK BRIDGE,** WOODBURY

Swamps and Caverns

SWAMPS

THE OKEFENOKEE SWAMP in southeastern Georgia is the 2nd largest freshwater swamp in the U.S. Islands, lakes, and prairies separate moss-covered forests. Okefenokee is an Indian word for *"trembling earth."*

The Okefenokee Swamp covers 438,000 acres (175,200 hectares). It's the place 15,000 alligators call home, sweet home!

Be careful–there are layers of peat deposits covered by grasses, shrubs, and trees–which is why the earth does indeed *tremble* when you walk on it! It's home to more than 1,000 different types of plants and animals!

CAVERNS

A maze of limestone caves runs through Pigeon Mountain in northwest Georgia. One is Pettijohn's Cave, and another is Ellison's Cave which has Fantastic Pit–the deepest vertical pit in the continental U.S.

A *spelunker* is a person who goes exploring caves!

Swamps and Caverns

QUESTION:
• Which is the stalagmite?
• Which is the stalactite?

ANSWER: Stalactites are long, tapering formations hanging from the roof of a cavern, produced by continuous watery deposits containing certain minerals. The mineral-rich water dripping from stalactites often forms conical stalagmites on the floor below.

Animals of Georgia

Georgia animals include:

White-tailed Deer
Black Bear
Fox
Opossum
Raccoon

Alligator
Skunk
Squirrel
Rabbit
Beaver
Wild Turkey
Wild Boar
Fox

The opossum is North America's only marsupial (pouched mammal). An opossum may "play possum" and pretend it is dead to escape an enemy!

Animals

Take A Walk on the Wild Side

Visitors to Cumberland Island, one of Georgia's barrier islands, can see  many beautiful sights—an unspoiled maritime forest, a sparkling-clean beach, and the wild horses that roam the south end of the island. These horses are probably descended from those left by explorers from Spain in the 1600s.

You'd better make plans early, since only 300 visitors a day can see the wonderful sites of this Golden Isle.

"Misty" is the name of a famous wild pony. If you check your library, you can probably find a book to read about Misty!

Don't forget your camera!

Wildlife Watch

Birds

YOU MAY SPY THESE BIRDS!

Downy Woodpecker
Barn Swallow
Cedar Waxwing
Mockingbird
American Robin
Hummingbird
Northern Cardinal
Song Sparrow
Screech Owl
Swallow
Blue Jay

Wood Duck

Quail

Wren

Mourning
Dove

Tern

A hummingbird's wings beat 75 times a second—so fast that you only see a blur! They make short, squeaky sounds, but do not sing.

Birds

Brown
Thrasher

Insects

Don't let these Georgia bugs bug you!

Beetle
Cicada
Cricket
Dragonfly
Firefly
Honeybee
Katydid
Mayfly
Mosquito
Moth
Praying Mantis
Termite
Walking Stick
Weevil
Yellow Jacket

Bumblebee

Ants

Tiger Swallowtail Butterfly–State Butterfly
–Papilio glaucus–

Ladybug

Grasshopper

Do we know any of these bugs?

Maybe...Hey, that ladybug is cute!

Be sure and flutter by the Cecil B. Day Butterfly Center at Callaway Gardens in Pine Mountain. It's the largest glass-enclosed butterfly conservatory in the U.S! You can even visit the nursery!

Insects

Fish

Largemouth Bass

Smallmouth Bass

Bream

Rock Bass

Carp

Catfish

Eel

Sunfish

Pickerel

Shad

Rainbow Trout

Fish

Sea Critters

Shrimp
Shark
Crab
Oyster
Dolphin
Manatee
Porpoise
Turtle
Squid
Right Whale
Manta Ray
Jellyfish
Scallop
Clam

Bottlenose dolphins send messages to each other by whistling and squealing. They will help an injured dolphin get to the surface so it can breathe!

Sea Critters

Seashells

She sells seashells by the Georgia seashore

Auger Shell

Cerith
Slipper Shell
Worm Shell
Helmet Shell
Wentletrap
Janthina
Sundial Shell
Vampire Shell
Tusk Shell

Bubble Shell
Knobbed Whelk
Mussel
Oyster
Scallop
Cockle
Angel Wing
Shipworm

Periwinkle

Knobbed Whelk

State Shell

Moon Shell

"Tabby" was made from oyster shells, lime, sand, and water. It was a building material used by Spanish missionaries and Georgia's founders–and it was used into the 1800s.

Seashells

Coquina

Trees

TREEMENDOUS!

THESE TREES TOWER OVER GEORGIA:

Live Oak
Magnolia
Dogwood
Sweet Gum
Sassafras
Cypress
Pecan
Pine
Birch
Beech
Sycamore

Blackgum
Bay

Wildflowers

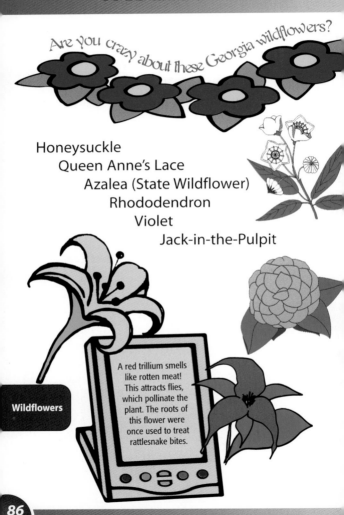

Are you crazy about these Georgia wildflowers?

Honeysuckle
Queen Anne's Lace
Azalea (State Wildflower)
Rhododendron
Violet
Jack-in-the-Pulpit

Wildflowers

A red trillium smells like rotten meat! This attracts flies, which pollinate the plant. The roots of this flower were once used to treat rattlesnake bites.

Cream of the Crops

Georgia's principal agricultural products:
The 3 Ps are specially "pointed out" for you!

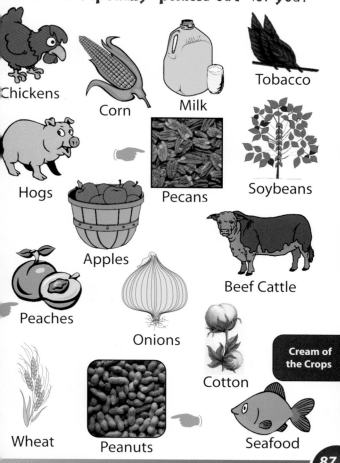

Chickens

Corn

Milk

Tobacco

Hogs

Pecans

Soybeans

Apples

Beef Cattle

Peaches

Onions

Cotton

Cream of
the Crops

Wheat

Peanuts

Seafood

First/Most/Big/Small

- 1828—First Native American newspaper, *The Cherokee Phoenix*, was published by Joseph Sequoyah in New Echota (historic capital of the Cherokee Nation).

- 1989—during National Peanut Month, the Penta Hotel in Atlanta built one of the world's largest peanut butter and jelly sandwiches. It measured 10x15 feet (3x4.5 meters). They used 500 pounds (225 kilograms) of peanut butter and 200 pounds (90 kilograms) of jelly.

- The world's SMALLEST CHURCH is in McIntosh County, south of I-95. The chapel, which still has services, measures 10x15 feet (3x4.5 cm), seats 12, and is open all the time so folks can always come in!

- The **BIG CHICKEN** is a famous Kentucky Fried Chicken restaurant landmark in Marietta. It's a 56 foot (17 meters) tall sheet-metal rooster that's even used as a reference point for traffic reports and by airline pilots!

- The **BIG FISH**—another local landmark stands beside another popular restaurant, the Atlanta Fish Market in Buckhead!

- The **BIG PEANUT**—On I-75, south of Ashburn, is the world's largest peanut! It sits in the center of a golden crown supported by a tower. Crown and tower stand 25 feet tall (7.5 meters)! What a Goober!

First/Most/ Big/Small

- Second only to Chicago, Atlanta has more shopping center space per person than any other city in the U.S.! Historic Underground Atlanta (part of Atlanta that wasn't torched during the Civil War) is now a popular "underground" shopping mall.

Festivals

Blairsville Sorghum Festival

Dahlonega's Gold Rush Days

Hahira Honeybee Festival

LAKE LANIER ISLANDS' GREAT PUMPKIN FESTIVAL

HIAWASSEE'S RHODODENDRON FESTIVAL AND GEORGIA MOUNTAIN FAIR

Cornelia's Big Red Apple Festival

CLARKESVILLE'S MOUNTAIN LAUREL FESTIVAL

Georgia Peach Festival in Fort Valley

National Black Arts Festival in Atlanta

Atlanta Dogwood Festival

Savannah Maritime Festival

Cherry Blossom Festival in Macon

GEORGIA RENAISSANCE FESTIVAL

Georgia Shakespeare Festival

Big Pig Jig (Barbeque Cooking Contest) in Vienna

NEW JAZZ FESTIVAL IN ATHENS

Arrowhead Arts and Crafts Festival in Macon

Patriotic Holidays

Calendar

Martin Luther King, Jr. Day, *3rd Monday in January*	Presidents Day, *3rd Monday in February*	Memorial Day, *last Monday in May*
Independence Day, July 4	Columbus Day, *2nd Monday in October*	Veteran's Day, November 1

Notes:

Special State Holidays

Robert E. Lee's Birthday, observed on the Friday following Thanksgiving

Confederate Memorial Day–April 26

Patriotic Holidays

Famous Foods

Georgia is famous for the following delicious foods!

Stewed Apples
Pecan Pie
Fried Chicken
Sweet Tea
Brunswick Stew
Barbeque
Girl Scout Cookies
Grits with Butter
Roasted Peanuts
Peach Cobbler
Claxton Fruitcake

Vidalia Onions
Boiled Shrimp
Deviled Crab
Scrambled Eggs
Biscuits and Gravy
Pork Chops
Sweet Potatoes
Fried Green Tomatoes
Fried Catfish
Black-eyed Peas
Collard Greens

Ya'll come and get it!

Business & Trade

Georgia's single largest industry is the manufacture of textiles– (cloth goods). Carpeting and cotton cloth are leading products. Other important industries include the making of products from peanuts,

fruits, and vegetables; mineral products, transportation equipment; chemical products; paper goods; and wood products.

Commercial fishing is important to Georgians living on the coast.

Atlanta is a very busy convention center!

Tourism is big time for the people of Georgia!

YA'LL COME!

Banks used to issue their own notes as currency, or money. Louisiana banks printed $10 bills known as *Dix*, which is French for the number ten. This paper money became known throughout the southern states as "dixies."

The word "Dixie" was later used to denote the entire South.

My First Book About Georgia by Carole Marsh
America the Beautiful: Georgia by Zachary A. Kent
From Sea to Shining Sea: Georgia by Dennis Brindell Fradin
Unique Georgia by Tom Barr
Let's Discover the States: The Southeast by the Aylesworths
Portrait of America: Georgia by Kathleen Thompson
The Georgia Experience by Carole Marsh

COOL GEORGIA WEBSITES

Georgia Fast Facts and Trivia
www.50states.com/facts/georgia.htm

Kids Page—Georgia History and Facts
209.144.138.98/tourism/index_kids.html

The Georgia Experience!
www.georgiaexperience.com

Historical Documents
www.atlhist.org

Georgia State Symbols
www.sos.state.ga.us/museum/html/state

Georgia
Glossary

GLOSSARY WORDS

abolitionist: a person opposed to slavery

colony: a region controlled by a distant country

constitution: a document outlining the role of a government

diorama: a scene in miniature reproduced in three dimensions by placing figures before a painted scene

emancipation: to be set free

frigate: a fast, heavily armed, naval vessel of the late 18th and early 19th centuries

immigrant: a person who comes to a new country to live

revolution: the overthrow of a government

secede: to voluntarily give up being a part of an organized group

terminus: either end of a railroad line

torrential: a violent downpour of rain

unrequited: unsatisfied

Georgia
Spelling Bee

ere are some special Georgia-related words to learn! To take
Spelling Bee, have someone call out the words and you spell
them aloud or write them on a piece of paper.

SPELLING WORDS

Appalachian	Honeybee
Atlanta	Kennesaw
Button	Moderation
Charter	Mound
Chattahoochee	Nacoochee
Cherokee	Oglethorpe
Creek	Okefenokee
Ducktown	Piedmont
Emancipation	Sautee
Etowah	Savannah
Granite	Spaghetti
Grizzard	Vidalia
Hartsfield	Whale

I'll bet you
got them
all right!

Spelling
List

ABOUT THE AUTHOR...

CAROLE MARSH has been writing about Georgia for more than 20 years. She is the author of the popular Georgia State Stuff series for young readers and creator, along with her son, Michael Marsh, of "Georgia Facts and Factivities," a CD-ROM widely used in Georgia schools. The author of more than 100 Georgia books and other supplementary educational materials on the state, Marsh is currently working on a new collection of Georgia materials for young people. Marsh correlates her Georgia materials to Georgia's Quality Core Curriculum. Many of her books and other materials have been inspired by or requested by Georgia teachers and librarians.

About
the
Author

EDITORIAL ASSISTANT EXTRAORDINAIRE: BILLIE WALBURN